dwelling

an anthology

by Samantha Keston

Copyright © 2024 Samantha Keston

All rights reserved, including the right to reproduce this book, or portions thereof in any form. No part of this text may be reproduced, transmitted, downloaded, decompiled, reverse engineered, or stored, in any form or introduced into any information storage and retrieval system, in any form or by any means, whether electronic or mechanical without the express written permission of the author.

ISBN: 978-1-917601-34-4

dwelling

When I was a child I was given a small turquoise ring binder file by an extraordinary lady, who you will meet later on in the piece entitled "Just One Day Too". On the front was printed "The Personal Anthology of ..." and beneath that was a small square of plastic into which the anthologist should slide his or her name. My treasured anthology followed me around for many months and became a huge source of enjoyment. My mother regularly worked long into the evenings, and a patient family friend who stayed with us would spend many after-supper hours throwing titles at me and I would proudly deliver my literary responses and receive generous encouragement. Mum was a mine of knowledge in the area of children's poetry and funnily enough when I eventually showed her my folder she took great interest in "The Swing". She asked a few questions about it and I floundered. She knew. It wasn't mine at all, but the published work of Robert Louis Stevenson. I learnt early that plagiarism didn't get you far. I was so humiliated that I didn't write much for a while, but I look back on the hobby with a sense of nostalgia.

What was so wonderful about the anthology? It was indeed a place to dwell, somewhere to squirrel away your ideas, but unlike a diary perhaps someone else might get something from the ideas within them too. Trying to express a thought, an idea - it's something that has never actually left me.

the (potential) function of poetry

The poem,
the po-em,
a landing place,
a stone
touching down to share the sentiment
of yes, I know,
I knew you.
You make me melt.
I see your hurt.
Your heart is art.
You left me for dead,

Hear me out:
a poem is shorter than a film,
takes less time than a show,
less shoe leather than a gallery,
and can have you drunk for free
while you sit home drinking tea.

Go write one,
or two,
or three—

Go publish your anthology.

table of contents

dwelling I
the (potential) function of poetry II

story
clearance 3
freepost 5
space and love 7
cacophony 9
winners losers 12
tarantula 15

lockdown
a village 19
worrying about every betty 21
sunflower 24
treading water 26
for the world we are missing where do I sit to grieve you? 29

family
journey 33
grandfather's footsteps 36
holi-daze 37
fathers day 40

the true meaning 43
the future is rosie 44
a love letter to hughenden 48

dwelling

peter pan and wendy 51
gods waiting room 55
why just one day? 57
just one day 59
just one day too 63
jumper 66
there are angels 68
chair 70
wanted 72
don't need to know 74
smelly-vision 79
for tombstone tim - the man at the corner shop 83
i try 84
buses 86
folly 87
forensic 89
crouching from wizards 98
heart beat - a song 101
from a glass bottom boat 103
the place we used to know - a song 105
gold silver bronze 107

story

clearance

Suki drags a ball and chain
out of the 4x4.
She trips, then
limps into the charity shop
with all
her old ideas.
Inside,
the skylight holds to account
batches of comics,
tired teapots,
and a woman—
her motherly hips
dried up—
who sits here
recording the passing detritus
with a wobbly wrist,
while dreaming today
of giving out parking tickets,
her twitching eyes peering
over the mask
that protects Suki from her
rich and garlic emphysema
and the gift aid stamp
and the rules.
Her jam lip, stooge

in hot pink hot pants,
breathes in and
dives
twenty feet deep
into the ocean
like Jacques Cousteau,
and surfaces
with treasured
keys to the 4x4.
Suki points out the gold bullion
and goes to the park for a '99.

freepost

I am trying to post a letter to my future self.
I am freefall into the rectangle
and awaiting the postman to carry me for sorting.
I am alone in here.
I'm nose towards the dusty bed
and laughing,
sprinkling old leaves like confetti into the vacant air.
And while you sit obedient in your smallholding,
my letter is unstamped.
I am legs akimbo,
dressed in shorts.
Blood rush and alive.
One shoe on, one off.
Freefall, freepost.
The words on the letter
tattooed with indelible needle on my soul
that assure me I will know myself
when I meet myself again.
Which I do.
Waking. Tumbling out. Thank you, postman.
Nice shoes, but your laces need replacing.
Long legs. Sorry. Did I scare you?
Hot palms.
Rubbing ash from the lifeline.
Wisdom.

I meet myself on the gravel and try to stand up.
My Bambi knees are schoolboy grazed.
You are tall. You help me to my feet.
Freepost.

I walk down the familiar street, hand in hand with myself.

space and love

Bernice loves to dig at things
with two long needles
that vary in size
according to the weather
or the day of the week
or her fluctuating hormones.
Today, as she is tying off a Bee stitch,
she picks a hole in her tongue
and spews dangerous words
into a cooling cup.
They are left on the mantel by the hearth
for human consumption,
but heat doesn't evaporate there,
and the room fills fast.
Furious steam becomes a facial spa
where she leans over the bowl
with a towel on her hair,
and the spa opens her pores
while out pour her feelings—
Beginning with dangerous words,
then harsh statements,
mediocre thoughts,
and finally, with the lightness of loving kindness.
A pool of butterfly kisses
that barely touch the bowl

falls as beads
like dewdrops,
leaving her empty
and ready for reconstruction.
"So tell me",
says the hazy mirror,
"What do you want me to reflect?"
"Layers of concrete,
peanut butter,
foundation,
then soil,
and cacao,
dreamy syrups,
heartwarming tea,
and scones.
For a kind conversation,
tissues for a friend,
warm breath for a pillow,
down for comfort,
and a newspaper for reference.
A match to ignite a spark,
Some colours—
emerald and topaz,
white for stillness and a song,
a small cash donation for the arts,
and the handle for a Tic Tac Toe,
and a space
for love."

cacophony

The man
whose life is
to tear the stubs
to Crown Jewel attractions
sighs,
furloughed—
sentiment merged
with mess in sobriety,
carnage in his disappointed sky
once blue.
He too used
to take a ticket
on the TFL
and now sits home
with a silent swell
of the news
that reminds us of Diana.
No space today
to say
that everything is
going to be
okay.
A damaged sky,
once filled positive
with eager narrative,

now bursting
carmine lip,
blue blood,
long curdled drip drip
and darkest tones
of slinging mud.
Today a pouring pan
of burning milk
spills onto wounds.
Two weeping hearts
of stiff lip sovereignty.
Breaking days
brought together
through vaccine celebration,
now united,
fighting discord—
ironic sharp
as the world remembers
their Diana,
who watches wise
and in pain,
perfect, pure,
poised
but equally helpless,
elegant in long robe death,
cold,
eternal,
stagnant.
Changing of the guard

left lost to low mood sleep
as the media rats rip
the groping tape,
as all those regal wounds
now open weep.
The golden mimes may return
this summer
to Covent Garden square,
but laughter
remains brokered.
Diana cries silent,
"Darling, save your brutal anger."
Bitter words
she mouths, muted.
And the furloughed man
whose life is to tear the stubs
to the Crown Jewel attraction
stays home,
listening in on his wireless,
and he carries on
wrapping his Christmas wishes,
bought online in March,
while no one else sees love.

winners losers

In corn
two oblivious torsos half naked
cut silhouette into a farmer's field
both warm and honey limb
she never leaving.
Snap. You lose.
He already left her
sandblasting her breath
with a flurry of poppies.
And then he met Ruth
who pulled open chickens
with two huge forks
at a feast of boiled and fat
grit-eyed potatoes from an allotment,
each paddling in the gravy with thyme
and a little piece of breast
and a wishbone.
I win.
It was a strange thing to wish for
but when such an old boy tells you to dig up a box
you do it—surrender.
Wishbone. I lose.
There was still blood
on the handle of the silver casket.
He took his cloth,

rubbed his glass emotionless
across forty years
and described the girl in the corn
and soil turned and poppies sprung.
The old boy wiped at the blood
on the handle of the silver casket
and held up a mirror on his marriage.
He shrugged emotionless and said
"That one was at home with the maggots."
He had, duty bound, visited her
at the yard behind the works.
There he painted like in blood and gravy
and imagined old potatoes
fat as her thighs
inside the box
that were crusted with blood
a stale pool
like jam,
like on the handles.
Inside it was dried up.
Just empty
like a window on their marriage.
1945
In the corn
a pair
half naked smiled
and animal
cut silhouette into the farmer's field
oblivious.

Their torsos, as one,
smashing into the whipping crop.
Wishbone.

tarantula

On the corner of the parade,
Double date?
You smile. Teeth
Like an advert.
"Sure."
Your fingers are like
Spaghetti forks;
You wipe them in your lap
Under the posh white tablecloth.
Kenny is awkward.
Sarah is
Watching her weight. Obviously.
You don't look like Sarah if you
Keep your carbs in.
"I need to go home," she fakes.
They leave.
You are warm.
Your skin is on my knee.
I am goose cold.
Later, you create a ritual
As you pour oil on Titania's bed.
A clock ticks loud as
You hold my gaze,
Streetlight flicking on,
Your hands fumble and twine,

And tickle, awkward.
Orange black orange.
You pull the blackout cord
And begin to scratch notches
Onto my glass frame.
We are pencils—
You are rubbing out your heart
Against my dignity,
Half hurting, half loving,
See-saw, see-saw.
Old curtains mis-hooked,
A fly,
And a grey string.
I want to go.
You're hurting me.
See-saw, see-saw.
Rough rug. The smell of parmesagna
And the metal of your fork.
You shunt.
In the doorway,
Oversized puppets
Print shadows on the wall.

lockdown

a village

You see clouds;
I see a village,
fair with women jostling
for cabbages and curd.
It's absurd, but I feel it
in the omnipresent air—
Not caring while the sky bursts
or turns to sleet,
and the rain is the pain
of not knowing and not caring.
At the end of the day,
it's as little as the spittle
of the shoeshiner's dribble.
Not to quibble, but it doesn't matter quite
if the cloud is there tomorrow,
and the sorrow busts the bank.
The middle marchers scuttle,
taking home all the eggs.
Under the cloud of forgiveness
sits a place I've never visited,
where all the little people
are just pins and needles in it,
their lives go on as day turns night,
and there's a date we've been given
to make things right.

But the government announces
that it's changed its mind again.
You see clouds in the sky;
I see villages beneath them,
deep oppressed by indecision—
an incision on the surface of the earth.
for what it's worth,
I'll sit here on my hilltop
to observe the shifting skies
while the people shake their heads
in all the wherefores and whys.
and the wise develop vaccines,
as I try to pay my taxes
with a deep breath on a dandelion clock.
The clouds shift out of sight.

worrying about every betty

Betty likes to hang upside down.
On the climbing frame,
her dress across her face,
she twists her knicker-lastic,
giving a knock-kneed peepshow
to the boys
on the roundabouts,
catching the breeze,
which she hopes God sees.
The cold metal pipes
are "muddied now with virus,
from the snip-snap crocodile jaw,
hair clipper boy from Manchester,"
says brother Hilary.
"Nah."
"'s true, 'cause he spat on his hands."
But Betty doesn't care—
It's upside downsy time for
fatsy thinsy,
lemon and lime,
In her hand-me-down dress
now turned to veil,
to kiss the boys
and make them wail.
A great big lick

of her 'coleslaw' lip
and catching teeth
on a piece that hangs like an
upsy downsy loose cotton hem,
hiding all the secrets in.
Eyes screwed tight
as day turns to night,
and the mocking cuts through
new clapping songs
set to the almost regular beat
of brother Hilary's stone
in the tread-of-his-shoe hopscotch.
She is hoping the boys don't go home—
not just yet.
Upsy downsy,
heads and shoulders,
shaking out the memory
of time before play.
"Why did mummy not eat today?"
Betty has an outy tummy button
that gathers fluff from Bear,
and she lies on the sofa on her bony back
to pick out the bits
with two chopsticks
Betty Blue Upside Downsy Explorer
in a world of wedding veils
and once upon a time,
she can try to forget things

like the sore she saw on nanny's leg
from the "maybe a fall".
Betty just wants this time to last forever
and for the chilly park air
to tickle her nostril,
and she wants it to rain
to wash away the morning
and the wee on her knickers
and to make her hair go curly,
and for the boys to see the colours,
and maybe,
just maybe, to
"Save me, Mr. God".

sunflower

"There shall be no more outdoor living,"
So I turn away from the huge and beautiful sash windows
to bury my head in government obedience.
I pick up a scarf and tie it to my head—
Blind Man's Buff,
pushing my glasses into my nose till they pinch,
tight, pressing against my face,
migraine tight,
glasses into my eyes,
cold and metal,
pinching into the bridge of my nose.
Tomorrow shall I still be blinded?
Will the tie on the back of my head
rub away my hair,
revealing me bald?
And even a hole that allows
me to scoop out all feeling?
My hand rips at the now—
Away it falls, allowing my fists to tear into my head.
And in the blackness—head, guts,
and flesh,
I find a long-lost symbol,
a key to youth
that was planted there
along with the sunflowers

the day I first saw Light.
I pull out the seeds
of the yellow smiling flowers
and turn my head to join the golden army.

I am here for the first time,
as a friend, not the officer—
the yellow flowering the sea of a million flowers,
pungent and united,
bold and stoic,
proud and lifted towards the light.
On Thursday it rains,
and the flowers drink.
I fill my cup, raise it to a thousand men.
On Friday I drink to the healthy nation,
mocking my futile years of self-glory.
On Saturday I dance
and change the colour settings on my screen
to heaven blue
and ash to mark the death of old ideas.
On Sunday I can sleep again.

treading water

I've joined a club
in a little village
called Treading Water.
It could save a life.
Here we learn
how to survive a minefield,
how to light our way with an oil wick,
how to navigate a danger bog,
and there are Boris bikes for sports days.
Maybe
we are forging decisions
in a vacuous void,
a deep tunnel where a bright light flickers
then dims.
Some nights overtaken by a flashing blue
with need on the end of freedoms.
At my club we've hit creative walls.
We've made great decisions—
we've made poor decisions.
We've stayed fit—
we've become unfit.
We are altered—
nothing has changed.
We've stayed the same—
and nothing stays the same.

Organisms shift,
we grow,
but in a stagnant pond
at the lockdown hills,
we can both stop
and continue.
How to explain time
to a walker
when it passes so slowly
to a metronome
gathering dust at an easy pace,
impossible to bear in isolation—
collected and connected
in experience and thought.
We are alone
together.
We are together
alone.
Humbled by the tears of isolation
We grow softer,
our connective tissue fragile,
but it's there
if you look
deep into the void.
Under the sea life changes.
The corals are best untouched.
Wolves can go a week without food.
We can survive without the feel of hand in hand.
February will not be spirit broken—

send love token.
We are changed
but the same.
We are humans in a club
in a little village
called Treading Water.

for the world we are missing, where do i sit to grieve you?

Caged in absence
in a silent night,
sleep broken by passing light
that signals that life is not alright.
Our sky too black to see the constellations,
emptiness too infinite to trust its end will come.
Where is the edge of pain?
As silent as birds gone south for winter warmth,
migration tempting in this lockdown mess
that leaves art fragile,
apparently untenable.
We hold memory in this space
of shattered dream and desperate news
to punctuate flaw and ask for your forgiveness
that we the people did not catch the fall.
I cannot see the stars tonight,
envelop'd in a cloak
of velvet black.
But sleep shall be the keeper from this fight
until a golden key of spring
is gifted back in light.

family

journey

I see you on the Circle line
dressed in abundant brown hair shining so bright you
know you might be Jesus
and your cheap guitar sits close to your chest
holding all the dreams in

I know your shirt will have lost a button
I've met you before.
You take up a seat
Get comfortable
your legs don't need it but it's going to be quite a journey
before kids come along
and then some

The train is an old one
It runs loud and rattles
which accentuates your youth
and stops
and starts up
A few jolts
yes I'm alive

life
You are going somewhere cool but it's not clear where

I follow you and your dreams across ten thousand days
and nights and the hope has never wained
Just rattled
This boy
Hair now silver in the plug hole
A cheaper one would have done us
a mortgage
A smaller one would have helped the hairline
a mound of brown unopened post
A smaller one would have been fine
To give space to dreams we permitted to be flattened by
societal strain
that wasn't offered a seat
But took it anyway
There's been a lot of honey and home soaked porridge
On the line from boy to father

filled a house with matey laughter
Baked bread
Got stressed
Gone to bed
Got dressed undressed
Never truer than the day we chose our children
And those teeth fought with those eyes
And said this might be quite a journey
But I'll do my best.
The train keeps going and nobody gets off but your guitar
has gone

And in its place is a photograph of your grown up daughters
Their eyes filled with hopes and dreams
Eyes bright with adventure as they board the tube and grab a seat
And I shout out not to waste the pigment in your hair
And the spring in your step
Because I'm now trying to
Turn back the clock.

grandfather's footsteps - lodz, poland

In memory of Grandpa, Matthew Rose.

As only a leaf should fall,
fear of failure is now futile.
It's time to turn back the blanket of perfection
and live as we intend.
Never more a promise of tomorrow,
once witness to tracks of gas and ash.
Today is their tomorrow,
In the end - and our ears,
descendants of a thousand silent stoics,
no playground stone throw,
no hopscotch winner—
Witness to a life where childhood grew thinner,
Disease at the root,
and a memory past.
remember the purpose
before we are lost.

holi-daze

Six in the morning,
and the sun is coming up
on just another old
weekend of holi-day.
The light shards shining in
are telling me it's going to be—
have to be—
a world-war bright-eyed, in-it-to-win-it
Proud-we're-winning day.
Because the sun doesn't know,
and the clouds will never know,
and the walkers 'compass will never show
that it's not just another happy, upbeat, chilly holi-day.
This is the time when the sun let us down;
This is the day we pulled the curtains down;
This is the day when systems shuttered down—
On any day being just another ordinary
satursundaymonday.
there's now no such thing as a normal May bank holiday.
The adventures keep us going,
and the days keep turning,
and the friendship ever flowing,
overflowing as the days
turn to months
and the years

into more.
The banks still shut,
and the walkers still walk,
and the bell keeps ringing,
and the birds are still singing,
and the children ever-growing,
and the lambs still frolic.
and the laughter keeps us going—
and going,
and it's
…and it's just not a normal live-your-life-not-caring
kind of life in our house anymore.
I'm proud of my children and the adventures they choose,
and I burst with pride at the conquerors of battles others lose.
I grow twenty feet as my sister moves forward
on a battle she's not losing, and the strength she shows to all.
I feel like I'm sitting in my dad's old apple tree,
and I'm sure that he's proud
of the growing family.
The summers still surround us,
though the tree is just a memory,
and Rosie's fruit is there too—
a sign of solidarity.
The world is ever spinning,
and we're all just passing through it,
guiding generations by the way we're talking to it.
There's no such thing as winning,

and the end is the beginning.
With pride, strength, and dignity, we will continue too.
So go, go, go big sister; hang on in there, brother Rob.
Use the strength your reboot gave you, and keep
fighting—never stop.
We'll clasp the gang around you,
and with heightened love surround you.
We are here and all around you
Through the Bank Holi-daze.

fathers day

Let me tell you about my dad
because chances are
that you and I met

long after my dad stopped
swivelling me round
in his favourite
leather chair

long after his pipe
was put away
and the cigar box became a place
To keep our pennies

long after the comfort of a seat on his lap

long after he smirked wanting to be liked

long after we put away his checkered trousers

pocket full of loose change

let me tell you of the man so generous
the man quiet and honest

the man who took a back seat
to watch everybody shine.

Let me tell you of the man
too quiet to tell you
he was self made
and proud of his boat with a hole in
of his jacket and his tie
of his discovery of Pavarotti
and his love for the family.

Thank you dad for your quiet generosity
I miss you especially right now but
we have missed you now for so long
I can't even remember your tone,
but I do remember your stoop
and your smile
and your shrug.

Because
nothing
nothing
can be so important

that it can't wait til tomorrow.
and so tonight
after a day of
a little too much

I can rest,
safe in the knowledge
that dad - you would agree.

the true meaning

What do you want for Christmas?
I asked young Dom, dressed in blue.
"A happy surprise," came the smiling retort—
At six, nearly seven, he knew.
It doesn't really matter what you ask for,
And matters even less what you got,
Because after the fun and frivolity,
The paper is all forgot.
But the part that can never quite leave you,
When the days travel on into years,
Is that friendships grow strong and reprieve you—
There's laughter and sometimes there's tears.
As I sat at our table this evening,
Aware of the things that we've seen,
I couldn't help pause for a moment
To ask what the whole thing can mean.
For Rob and for Ellie and Caro,
Who've fought back some battles all told,
There'll come a new year very shortly
With a tiny new hand now to hold.
I am grateful for friends who stand by us,
I hold close my dear family and friends,
And the snap of the cracker reminds me
Of the nonsense on which one depends.

the future is rosie –
in those pages

On the walls of the bookshop
live a thousand stories
holding a million ideas
each celebrated
most unique
and certainly special

They record the many years of
toil and vision
and are a momentary
holding in time of an idea.

The last time I stepped into one of these shops…

-these ships where a-sail for hours and hours
past covers
and titles
and names
we float
and look for the ones we know
(and sometimes do!)
like an old familiar friend…

I felt more "at sea".

A bookshop, whether we buy a slice of the story or not,
is a search for an old friend
a light
a crystallisation
of what we think we know

But this
this beautiful
beautiful
beautiful evening
the walls stepped back
the friends stepped in
It was 'mounded'

to honour the journey
of one most special author

And her pen touched the paper
and her story
once again
touched hearts

And I was deeply
deeply proud
of my sister
and my family

and the wider family she has created around
her story.

HER story.
The story of a journey,

held by the hand
by her three beautiful children.

Last night she found a feather -
Not any old.

The feather.
The one that finds you
to remind you that
she is here too.

Rosie was at the party.
She got everyone there.
She gave the stage directions.

Now I'm sure she's saying-
Open the pages.

Read her mummy's story.
You won't put it down.
She will tell you it how it is.
and you will understand
this world a little better

Because you, like all of us
Because of my sister

Shall know what does and doesn't matter.

I am in awe
of my sister
and her story
and her son
and her two daughters.

the one who poured you a drink last night
to welcome you

and the little girl
who dropped a feather.

a love letter to hughenden

You give water to replenish the soul,
in a path that's never still,
broken only by the boulder
that's become a casual friend.
There are ducks to tease my dog,
and he in turn smiles
to thank Disraeli.
I watch his four legs scurry,
to chase ducks and smile at freedom,
as I share air with an elder man
whose dog gifts me a saliva'd ball,
and smiles so sweet
as I can remember being seven.

Here is my ode to the joy of early rising,
observed today with words.
An only annoyance in a selfish game—
of nose in ground, and sprint, and solitude—
yet even so, I take home phrases
to remind me after
of today's journey
into the spirit of being alive.

dwelling

peter pan and wendy

You and I were never short of words;
We had an opinion on everything,
Spoke in code or glance,
and spent long summer nights
putting the world to rights—
What we called "pah-ing"—side-splitting laughter
at anything light.
We spoke a language connected
by simply catching an eye.
These were halcyon days
when only a little homework or a chore
might need to be done,
when the two King Charles
might need a belly rub,
or we might be asked to wash the car
and end up soaked, hunting for towels.
Your garage was my Narnia,
filled with Yogi Bears and life-sized cutouts,
and Diddi was my rock.
I am sitting in your bedroom at Clarefield Drive—
Two one two one to the neighbours—
"Can you hear me?"
We are playing on a CB,
dancing to Rainbow.
You are dressed in a white baseball jacket
with green writing.

We knock out scripts with no agenda,
and when I go home,
you watch Cabaret,
reciting the words from start to end.
You turn up an hour later
for "drama" with my mum.
You are her brown-eyed boy.
We rehearse a play—
The Bad Seed.
You play a psychopath;
My American accent is too shocking, so again we laugh
and laugh.
We improvise for hours—
an extension of childhood play,
but yours is serious because it leads to theatre,
and it's important.
Everyone loves Marnie, but you are oblivious;
You have auditions to attend,
scripts to write,
and we have things to laugh at.
The roller disco is loud;
You attend both sessions
to practice your moves.
My only dread is that another success,
another distraction, will take you away from me
or ruin our holiday
that we've paid for.
The risk we take—we go without you once again
for a screen test in Bristol.

You get a yes, and I a no,
so I lose you again.
SWALK—months missing you,
The Silent Twins,
Then, a BBC drama.
I'm 16 and living in a fairytale
that only shatters when our roller skates
at the roller disco give way to the city,
to be a singing train.
Several years later, we are still soul buddies,
connected now by airmail.
I call your darling brother
on a number from a letter you sent
with a Christmas gift.
You are in LA,
I ask you to wait in for a parcel—
It's quite big and can't go through the letterbox.
It's me - I arrive in the city of dreams,
and we continue to laugh for three long weeks
as you dress in army gear for castings
and we party with Kids from Fame in Beverly Hills.
We are joined by Andrew,
who drives us to Phoenix,
where I get sunstroke and am very sick.
My laughter returns and is simple,
but yours hides your worries
that one day you might be on a podium
sharing your stories.
not long after, this comes true—

you are nominated.
You are my childhood hand in hand.
My barometer,
The Paul to my Cory,
The director of my only lead movie moment,
The only person who could make me share
my frozen Mars bar.
The reason for my courage.
You did the things I dreamt of doing
You had the Christmases I wanted to have.
A gap of twenty years as lives are made
and pacts are broken,
and your passing has made heaven
a more welcome place for one day,
when we will be ready to meet again.
Dark years, pieces of the jigsaw—
A simple reminder of your fragility
that made you such a soul
as only angels are.
I was lucky to meet you and be able to call you
the holder of the key to my childhood.
"Some people," said J.M. Barrie,
"Never grow up."
And you shall forever be
The Peter Pan to my Wendy.
RIP

god's waiting room
(On when we pass)

God's waiting room
In a queue
that formed
I want to say today
but what is that anyway
she makes a friend
he shares a story
of a situation
termination
new beginnings
middle
endings
They laugh
those energies in that line
and sparks aligns
taking making order
connection
reconnection
system load
overload
power surge
enough to send a bolt
of light
You told us

he might say
if he still needed
but doesn't
You told us to behave
to make an ordered line
so we would hold a halo up to Time
How were we so damned wrong?
The queue is a full month long
and he wants a chair
but stand he might
to keep sight of the electrical connections
at various intersections
Lighting strikes blue
Messaging earth or elsewhere
London
Delhi
Nairobi
all intersecting at this state
of heaven's gate
A queue
You.
Spark.
Quiet. Rest. Rest.
Spark rest.
Sleep. Blue sleep.

why just one day?

The ideas are pouring out of me. It's the strangest feeling after the most arid period. The bigger project has been "on hold" as I wait to do some booked in work on reshaping it and I gave myself permission in the meantime to do nothing. It's given me time to rethink.

The thing I have become aware of is the self censoring, and this is why I'm now spewing unedited pieces onto the blog here. It's a part of a process, an unblocking. While the piece I care so much about continues to be about creating the finest result I can achieve, there is satisfaction in sharing some smaller ideas. I would once have kept these back. They are only exercises, an hour long at most, but like a student artist I need to throw some ideas out there, and then chuck them away. There is an unburdening in this process.

So this piece is the entree to an idea about getting "Just One Day" to spend with someone again. Perhaps in this story I might, or I did, or perhaps we one day will. Who knows!

It's an exploration of the idea that there are always things left unsaid. I suppose this process is about trying to shift that narrative so that things are said. In this case I won't get the chance to speak to these people again.

We all have people in our lives who "meet us" in some way, and who change us by knowing them. They don't always know it and we don't always get to thank them. This piece I dedicate to some of my people.

This "opener" is steered by my late childhood friend, whose impact on my formative years was unquestionable. Sadly there were too many words unsaid so perhaps this why he is leading this piece at a time when I am grappling to share my most authentic voice. The longer version I believe would visit perhaps a handful of my greatest influences, in an imagined conversation for Just One Day.

just one day

There was something daunting about today. She felt it on waking. Today she wanted it to be a good day. She would give it a go. Every day was a new chance. The opportunity to start over. Refresh. Delete even. She wanted to delete yesterday. It had been too hard.

When you bury someone there is supposed to be closure. An end point. A chance to move on with life, but something wasn't working. She didn't think he was properly gone. There had been no chance to say goodbye and however many times she told herself it would get easier, it wasn't getting better. "It's only been a day." The babble that was usually pretty helpful but today she wanted to thump the next person who trivialised it. Was it ever going to get better? She knew that grief wasn't the same for everyone, but she honestly didn't know how she was going to get through this.

This is my story. So I shall change the "she" to I and speak from the heart because if we don't there is simply no point.

This is my grief. And I want to introduce you to my first visitor. This sounds like a chat show. And I wish it was. But it really isn't because the room is silent, save for the beating of my heart. Only mine.

My visitor is…. No longer a beating heart of his own. His heart never recovered. He hadn't treated himself well so it was likely to be in a sticky state even if it did work. But this is all immaterial because he lost his life. But here he was.

"D'you want a drink?"
"I'd better not."

"I meant tea. You can have something a bit stronger, you know, if you want."

"I don't actually know".

"Right. Well unless you've missed something in the last couple of months, you'll remember."

I looked straight back at him. His eyes were the ones I remembered from when we were kids. His chuckle too. He looked better than he had for a while although not dissimilar in stature.

"Chuck us a cookie."

I wanted to hug him. To say how gutted I was that he was gone but actually wasn't sure he was gone, or was here right now or… wait.

I walked over to the fridge and grabbed a can of San Pellegrino.

"Blood orange" I said.

"Nice" he replied.

When you lose someone. Correction. This is happening to me, not to you. Sometimes I'm caught up in the moment and I go to ring you, and you're not there.

"Yeah. I mean no".

"D'you know what I mean?"

"Sort of, I mean. No. Haven't a clue."

It's a painful thing. Empty.

"It doesn't matter."

"Of course it matters. If it didn't matter we wouldn't be here now."

"You're not.

I look across the road at the house opposite. I'm checking in on my sense of perspective and today seems to be like any other. There are a few of them in there. They are like student sort of age and there's a lot of coming and going and sometimes a bit of hanky-panky and frivolity but nothing that looks too serious or worth writing home about.

I felt jealous of those young girls. I wished I could feel like that again. Carefree and a bit stupid.

The word "Stupid" poured off my tongue.
"Who you calling stupid?"

*

My friend had left us very suddenly. He wasn't at an age when people tend to die but he had abused his body and it was kicking back. I hadn't seen a lot of him, for what I felt was good and conscious reason, and in self protection. He was making what I felt to be poor decisions and I found this uncomfortable but didn't want to reach out. It seemed I was going to get a second chance. To talk to him. I wonder if he might listen this time. Did he even know he was dead?

"I wonder if you know how many people you hurt?"
"In a lifetime?
"No. Well actually, yes!
"If I could tell you just one thing that might change the past?
"It doesn't work like that."
The future then, I thought. Just leave a note!
You hadn't left a note, but you HAD left a letter. It was written in royal blue ink and onto glorious parchment paper that I reckon might have been your mums. You wouldn't have spent money on that stuff. The paper you spent your money on was roll ups and that had always disappointed me.

Your letter was beautiful and you read it to me now, again. You know I've been numb since your passing but hearing you say the words instead of trying to remember your voice and the floodgates opened. It was the first time I'd felt anything, except for the shame of letting you down. So it shook me up. It went like this.

"I want to go."

"Can we stop this and take the bikes out?" You loved your bike.

"It's ok. You go. On your own."

You decided not to go but I could tell you were keen to experience the wind on your skin again.

"Any idea who ended up with my bike?" he asked.

I shook my head. "We can go look for it?" I offered.

Walking hand in hand with my friend. Not lovers. Just friends. I felt oddly complete, and proud to have him with me. I could feel his warm body near to me as we shared the kinship that was broken in our twenties and I could hear his...breath.

There should be no breath. You can't breathe again as well - surely?

just one day too

She had been here before. Her wide hat larger than life as she stepped into the drawing room again if only for just one day.

I had always felt her to be someone who had been here before, even when I was a young child, because her choice of dress was far out of the ordinary, blacker than night velvet, a brooch tightly clasping at the neck her most glorious victorian lace. "Darling." She delivered in the biggest most eloquent outburst. "Darling little lady you haven't changed one little bit." She squeezed my cheeks with her warm fingers, expecting them to be childhood chubby. It was odd to feel those fingers on my face, odd to hear these words from the mouth of a woman who had without any question been an annual influence in my young life. Once a year, as sure as the changing seasons, or British Summer Time, as certain as the night sky, Frieda would appear at the door of my home - a glorious apparition who would celebrate her friendship with my mother through a small amount of paid business and then, as sure as the sunsetting over our garden she would be shuffled off to the west wing for a good night's shut-eye, and to write up her certificates in the biggest, most glorious flourish of her calligraphic hand.

Frieda was something of an enigma, a mentor, a guide, and more than she would ever know, and here she was returning to show me that while the seasons might come and go, and life and death happens in between, there are constants, and this British eccentric was one of those. Frieda was special and I had known it at our first encounter, but why was she visiting me now?

She had had a period of rest, that was possibly 50 years long and it clearly suited her because today she looked even more glorious and wonderful than I had remembered her. She handed me a tube of lightly dusted chocolate almonds, and my heart sung. The same treat. She remembered how much I loved them. The cycle of her visits had stopped short and I was never sure why. Perhaps she had become too old to manage the train journey from her faraway home. Or maybe she had died. Nobody told me about these things so I had assumed she must be gone.

She was no different after these years. "Sweetheart" her voice like lush gravel. "Some of us never die and she spouted the words of the bard - the seven ages of man, then proceeded to throw off her glorious black cape with the gayest abandon. "How I missed your family my sweet darling and not being sniffy but I've been watching the changing seasons and there is something a little lacklustre going on here. Is it your mother? Don't tell me I've missed her?"

"Yes. She's gone."
"Darling nobody lasts forever" she annunciated "although let me tell you something. There are words that transcend time herself. Poetry. Purple prose, recital, theatre darling, darling darling darling darling darling don't get me started." She didn't stop for air. "I shall be here for an eternity and they've only given me one day. When the clock strikes twelve…" I imagined a black velveteen pumpkin.

I looked out of the window. The moon was full but it simply served to light the night sky and I was far from afraid. It was heavenly. Her return to my life seemed oddly inevitable and I was grateful for it. I looked at her, unable to take my eyes off this magnificent being. I tried to count the wrinkles in the way I had once learnt to count the rings on a tree. There was so little form, just hundreds and hundreds of fine lines.

"Frieda I'm not sure why you chose to come today but you might want to know you always had a special place in my life."

"I know I know" she beamed back at me and her piercing blue eyes glinted.

jumper

It was a silly thing
Stopped me from shopping.

I am in a changing room
Just a bunch of shirts
That I quite like.

It's just a mindless afternoon
A few hours escape
Nothing serious.

"I'll keep the jumper here for you
To try after"

They only allow three items in the dressing room
At once
"That's fine
I know I like it already"

Shirts rejected
She passes me the jumper
The colour
Well yes
I like it
But can I justify it. I like the buttons.

But they are tricky …

And
Wait
It's not for me.
I've picked up a jumper
That I would have bought for mum

It would have been for Christmas.
Beautiful buttons on it.
I swallow.
And the bluebirds.

The rest of the day is written off.

there are angels

"Just say you don't know."
This is what you told me
when I made a call
that wasn't yours
or wasn't right.
Sometimes in the space of not knowing
a moment occurs—
an unexplainable
where angels tread,
take over,
roll their sleeves and
take action.
Yesterday I was served by angels.
They had worked hard to find a clearing
but took me to a place I know
but angels rarely tread.
Here they held the door
and blocked enrolment,
taking me to meet a friend
I didn't know I didn't know
but knows so many that I do.
Mum, you did it.
You didn't say I'm here
but took me through a journey
into Narnia

with Lucy as your hero
and old familiar places.
Secure on the space,
you tapped my hand
and took me steps towards
a promised land.
I will be strong,
I've been saying,
I can do this.
Just breathe.
I can't.
You can.
Take my hand.
I do.
I know you have arrived
safely
and are at work with the angels.

chair

I sat with you yesterday
and the chosen chair was
more comfortable
so I could sit for longer
and even read a book you chose for me.

You know -
even on quieter days
you are pottering
sorting a corner of your castle
listing your groceries
like they might ever change
and stirring the Sweetex into the black.
Your spoon against the cup.
"I like this one" you say.

You never follow me home -
You are far too polite -
but my thoughts do
and try as I do to keep
the keeping on
you had me sit on a sofa
for three whole weeks of
in out in out,
checking I was still here.

Pinch me pinch me.
Can't feel much today
Tomorrow.
Yesterday.
But this has lifted now.

Today you are in the birdsong
fast and busy
looking about my garden hectic
nodding that at last we are taking
a little
more
care.

In the lead up to national holidays you are saying
"Deal with today - not the calendar you didn't set,
but thank you anyway.
Daffodils are fine.
Don't spend your money.

Watch out for magpies.
Troubles fade - let them be.
They will get bored.

You can smell history
even touch it
but you can't change it.

wanted

A poster in the doorway
of the old saloon
worn edges curly.
WANTED.
MISSING.
365

Your face on the poster,
upturned nose
a glint in your eyes
but centre stage.
You never
liked that
And nor do we.

The door swings open.
I do my best to swagger in.
The sheriff looks up eventually.
and I give my evidence
now thick with stagnant stories,
a film on repeat,
because you have nothing to add

It's been a year today.
Oh and

I miss you.
What can I say?

Memories of costumes
that held up the wall
the way you'd push up your nose.

The shuffle in the kitchen,
the rhythm of your steps,
the smell of pearl barley,
the telly blaring.

Your desk,
your notebooks
full of lists
your curious interest in schools that came and went,
and other people's palaces.

Even the olive oil smells of your skin.
I have begun to stir my coffee the way you did,

WANTED.
One in a million.
Just imagine if they found you.
just missing.

don't need to know

To be a writer we have to reveal the layers. I grew up in a house where we papered over the cracks. Things were not discussed. Nobody spoke to a child the way they might now. Children didn't need to understand the way the world works. They shouldn't enquire. Don't ask don't need to know. Don't Need to Know sits silent in the corner. Don't Need to Know is stifled. He watches as others pass through. Because they ask questions. And they grow. I watch as the ivy grows through the window. The window reveals only a little light. It's an old window that no longer opens. Don't need to know why. It just doesn't, ok? Because the wood has expanded. You don't need to know how that works. It just happens. When it's damp.

The house is damp. Especially today. The cold gets into your bones they say. It gives you arthritic joints. My family have those. I'm not sure if they always did, or if they came with the house. A huge mound of history. Iron gates. Strong enough to keep ideas out. And to keep a family in. We played tennis against that wall. Now it's no longer straight. Roots must have warped it. Or the wind. Or the kid in the summer who kicked it with his great big boots. Or God. God the Giant blew and Jack went to market with the cow and came home with the beans. My dad was like that. He took his books to market and came home with a box of artefacts and a receipt for his petrol. And a box of apples. Once my dad sat under that tree. We used to think he had forever. Then he began sleeping more and before long he slept so much under the tree that we used to call out DAD. Close your mouth before an apple falls in it. That apple did fall one day. Dad died. All apples fall. All dads die. Eventually. My dad did.

My mum didn't mention him. Don't ask. You don't need to know. If you don't ask you don't care and if you do ask you don't know so sometimes, just sometimes. The world was easier in a story. Stories had a structure. A beginning a middle and sometimes an ending.

There was once a house. It had a structure. It also had a story. A beginning and a middle. Don't ask about the ending. You don't want to ask because if you don't ask you don't care and if you do ask you might find out. A house begins as a single brick. And then another and another until it's a big box that keeps out the rain. It's not just that. It keeps us safe.

Like stories. Stories keep us safe. Especially if we create them. Then we control them. I give you the story of a house. It's a strange place - a house filled with art, and beauty. But what of love? Yes, love lives here too. It's a house of immense glamour. It radiates frivolity. Splendour. Pure unending riches. But if you look, it doesn't take a lot. If you look behind the curtain, through the window, behind the door. It's collapsing, a building in reverse like it must have its say, one moment at a time. Little by little. Wait. The bulging wallpaper.

She taps it. Tumbling falling brick. Like a house of cards, a poker game where the chips are down she tumbles, falling like Alice onto the flat earth of the rabbit hole beneath. "Don't Need to Know" holds onto the bar by the window. He assumes it is safe. The plaster is damp so don't need to know might not be as safe as he thinks he is. But don't need to know doesn't need to know because things like that just freak out kids, but it would be good if his mum told him gently not to lean on the bar. Just in case. The just in case came just too late and Don't Need to Know did take a fall, landing in a small pond of a terraced garden where it was summertime and a group of children sat, discussing What had happened to Lulu. They didn't notice Don't Need to Know because Don't Need to Know had spent so many years feeling invisible that he actually became transparent. Save for a flow of air, the terrace and the kids of local intelligentsia remained unaltered. They didn't need to know Don't need to know and don't need to know didn't want to trouble them.

So he sat, listening to the voices, accepting that he mattered very little, brushing his bruises. It wasn't the time to disturb his mum. She would ask why he was leaning on the window after lights out and he would have to explain that he heard children, even younger than himself, learning all the things that he might want to know, and he was just leaning on the window, minding his own business when the cement gave way. It was bound to happen at some point. Nothing lasts forever. Save memories, guilt, unused soaps and blocked plumbing. It wasn't likely that Don't Need to Know would get much sympathy so he sloped off, and went to find a roll of sticky tape to mend his broken knee he sat for a long while pulling the pieces of patio grit, one by one by one from his chafed and slightly ruddy kneecap. When Don't Need to Know brought this up the next day, Mum was bemused. You're making it up. You weren't even there. It was past six o'clock. You were long in bed. That's it. Don't need to know had dreamt it. Dreamt everything. That was all he needed to know.

In the gap between reality and fiction lies a great space for possibility and Don't Need to Know was fast becoming a ball of imagination. His bedroom became an Imaginarium filled with space for dreams and the same few books that he was fed, over and over by the likes of Robert Louis Stevenson, whose swing went so high into the air so blue that Don't need to know thought he should never come down. He watched the clouds shapeshifting across the small square of the sky and hoped for a bird to fly through his window and take him off to a new land. One where the hours passed more quickly and where he could perhaps learn just a little something so he didn't feel quite so stupid. It might be about animals or cookery and as he didn't have any animals except for an occasional visit from a fat grey kitten he decided to try a little baking.

With Mother as busy as she was he opened the cupboard and looked to see what might be in there. A larder of sorts. It held old plain flour, baking soda and glacee cherries. There were baking cards from another life so he had a little look for something with sticky cherries and found his way to an edition entitled Floury Fingers. He put on an apron, turned on the oven and then heard a noise. A small visit from a highly attuned mouse made all the difference. As the blender spun around and flour shot out in every direction, Don't Need to Know wished he knew just a little more about electricity. Should he turn it off and remove the mouse or … without further thought, Don't need to know was trying to save the life of a small woodland creature. His day was worthwhile. A true creative, he had combined his two thoughts. That of the cordon bleu chef and that of the animal saviour. This was significant. Something to contribute to the conversation at school. Don't need to know would sound like he had had a full-on weekend of amazing adventures. Nobody would need to know that his arm would need to be reconnected at the elbow, as long as he kept his blazer firmly buttoned.

It was fortunate that it was one of the cooler days of term. When your limbs are hanging off, quite literally it is useful to have someone take just a little interest in you. Don't need to know might have been called Don't make a fuss because his life seemed not to matter one iota. Nobody would notice that he wasn't doing games today. His face was always light in colour but today it was hard to tell whether it was pale green or pale yellow as his skin was hidden by the white flour that had shot out into the kitchen air during the cookery. Don't need to know had no interest in sport. Not any. Possibly as his level of fitness was below par at the time he had started his education he had fallen far behind and was now most certainly unable to learn the rules. He had once tried to play catch up by looking at the drawing of the netball court in Make Do and Mend, a 12 anthology set of encyclopaedias for children sporting some delightful drawings. The books took pride of place on the shelf and while they appeared terribly intellectual they were a good way to mask his ignorance as they included many, many pictures.

What you have read is the unedited outcome of a free write and I see I have created the foundations of a story. Don't Need to Know might soon become a real live boy.

smellyvision

It's 1976. A heatwave and I'm lying on my bed. It's a single, and I think at that time I have sheets that tuck in. This is before we went to an early Makro and came home with new fangled things called duvets. I remember it being pretty cold most of the time. I have, to this day, an unusually acute sense of smell and I'm lying there wondering what it might be like to invent a new kind of TV.

It's called Smellyvision and to try it out before the BBC might invest bucketloads of cash in my idea when I write to them. I had habit of contacting people - I own a Blue Peter badge for sending them my buttons, and spent Saturdays trying to all Noel Edmonds on Multicoloured Swap Shop to see if anyone wanted my broken Kerplunk. I also used to call the police from the call box in the "waiting room" at our house. My mother always said you had to go through the boredom threshold to come out the other side. I think in my case it went a little too far.

So, I'm lying there, thinking it would be a great idea to hire the ABC cinema, and to buy a lot of indoor plant water sprays from the garden centre which people can keep by their feet. Each bottle is numbered and ready to spray when a number comes up on the screen. The smells, let's just say, aren't likely to be from the Gucci Alchemist's Garden selection but are more in the nature of domestic smells like lawn cuttings, or manky stew bubbling, or maybe beans and diesel at a truckers cafe.

For those who know me well you also know this was a passing whim. My mother told me (even after 40 years in a committed career) that I didn't stick at anything for long.

While I know it not to be true I think she may have been referring to my racing mind that wasn't able to push through the mechanics of creating such dreams. I also dreamt up an indoor playground called The Beach but I didn't have an industrial unit. It was a little like the wave pools that kids love so much now, but mine offered limited ability to swim. It was just a beach, complete with tides, and the sounds and the smell of the sea and dirty great piles of sand to create sculptures that were rinsed down by the night shift. The lack of any interest in engineering let me down once again. I'm not sure how the hygiene police would have dealt with policing the children's wee.

Some years later - perhaps early '90's, I find myself at an exhibition. This time it doesn't smell of much, except perhaps some sweaty fabrics and dry ice, but from memory it's a Peter Greenaway installation although I may be wrong) but I recall being wowed by the interaction between actor/models and environment. Perhaps it was this that has been sitting quietly in my psyche and what inspired me to plan (a still unexecuted) installation on the theme of radical unschooling. I have the notes and was ready with the wish list of contributors, many of whom I had lined up. But something was stopping me. Perhaps the omnipresent fear of failure. I think at the time it wasn't the international nature of the project that was daunting, but I couldn't work out quite what I was trying to say. Then lockdown happened and the world became expert on the very theme. But the piece still sits in my head, and I can still picture the huge metal tree sculpture and the kids swinging from it at the premiere where the audience are sitting at wooden school desks.

Like it or not, I remain a quirky thinker.
Here is a collection of images, a curation that speaks to me of Mother.

I can't offer Smellyvision but you are welcome to pop into Boots and spray yourself with Blue Grass before viewing these images that I snapped in that cold September.

for tombstone tim
the man at the corner shop

Thanks for the extra candy.
Sorry I embarrassed you
when I rode my bike there
to buy my first pad
and asked you
to put my monthly
on the monthly.

You owned
the smell of ham.
You sliced it sliver thin
with your silver gadget machine
just for the asking.

Thanks for not telling my mum
that I put cherry-ade
on the account.
You called it "goods".

It's true.
You were good.

i try

i try.
"you don't try hard enough."
i'm exhausted from trying.
My foot hit the pedal
the day my mother died.
The fire went out.
Burnout.
The grate showed up
like tea leaves,
a pattern of the future
in the shell shock of our past.
Past -
Past life ready trodden,
the new path yet to trample.
We slash at nettles,
stinging our legs,
bare thighs, and hearts,
whiplashed through shock
of an ugly year,
Creating joy
and memories
while the show goes on,
and on -and on
making worlds smaller
but our craters taller,

perfecting their own destructive imperfection
past any resurrection.
No return. No
i know i'm not perfect,
but i try.
again, i try,
until the exhaustion lifts.
i commit to try.

buses

All the buses came at once,
to carry away what we held as ours—
A sow's ear, a silk purse,
and pieces of life
that even the sow would have
clung to, if he could.
So we did.
In the end,
a negotiation carved
by the hand of a hesitant craftsman,
left a residue of guilt
and carpets dented
with the weight of your history.

So I parked it.
No buses running today.
This life matters—
But we are only custodians,
holding these things for a fleeting time.

They make us feel
like we are special,
as if we laid the tongue and groove
with our own hands.

folly

You built castles
in the sky,
kept the title role
but took us high
on your adventures,
with James' sky hooks
on a peach.
A childhood
without a beach
traded in for
broken plates
and paper dreams,
and cities
and ice creams
built from pure imagination,
it is now too late
to beg an explanation
of a mother's motivation.
Perhaps of war or jealous whims,
or whatever else drove you
to build my life without
a litmus test.

Those rooms,
symbols of your treasures

fall into disarray
like my lonely evenings,
entrusted by the god of luck to you and dad.
As the carpet disintegrates
dust to dust like a childhood dream,
and lucy steps out of the wardrobe,
filth turns promise into pyre
and tomorrow into trash.

You chose this
not just for yourself,
but your rose-coloured days
were shared with our hoorays
who played your games
and climbed willing into costume
and danced to your bidding.

How do i forgive illusion
as we throw petrol on your musing
and the flames take my
puppet strings with them,
high past heavens gate?
It's too late
to begin a conversation.

forensic

I have developed a fixation with wanting to photograph and catalogue every part of my mother's house. The home I grew up in was the house my mother died in on September 16, 2023. At least, I believe this to be the case, although my gut, and it's a good one, tells me she died on September 12, 2023, of a broken heart.

September 12 would have been the day my brother turned 60, except that he sadly didn't make it.

I will no doubt share more about my brother later as I explore and excavate all that I know to be true. Perhaps through my findings and jolts of memory, I may be led, like in a story by Kit Williams, toward the explanations I am seeking.

Let's begin at the beginning. The beginning being the end. The end of life begins when I receive a call. I am with my husband and oldest daughter. We are in a field near home when the call comes. It's my sister. It's afternoon. I think. In fact, I am unsure. Yes, it's afternoon. My sister tells me the words I have known were coming for twenty years but was not prepared for: "It's Mum. She's dead."

Those words are shards. I hear myself scream into the silent air, and my legs begin to run, although I have no clue why. I am holding the lead of our dog. I run. I think we all run.

"NO", I bellow into the air.

I remember very little of the following hour but I recall arriving at my mother's home. I have little memory of the order of things but my other daughter also arrives, and my nieces also gather. My older brother does not attend. There are police at the house. One of them, white female, is very young and this appears to be her first exposure to death.

She knew about my mother's legacy.

"I wanted to come to your mother's school," she tells us to break the silence. Partly touched and partly confused, I wonder why a policewoman wanted to train as an actor. Is she simply acting this role in life? The pair talk to each other and agree that things are not straightforward. I wonder why.

They ask my sister to look at my mother's body. I have only seen her ankles. I don't want to see her eyes. My sister tells me that she holds her chest and one arm is behind her head. The policeman is concerned and asks many questions. I ask why there is a Monopoly set in the middle of the floor. My mother did not play Monopoly. I still have no idea.

I look inside the box, asking if there is something in there she needed us to see. There is not.

The days that follow are peculiar. This is an academic memory because I remember very little. I send hundreds and hundreds of texts to family and friends, but mostly to those my mother really influenced across decades. There is so much sadness in the replies and also a camaraderie that reminds me of who she was before those final moments—the ones that brought angry emails and conversations that made me turn my car around or forget where I was going.

I hope truly that whoever is next to inhabit her soul pitches up somewhere vibrant, because she would be wasted in the burbs. Her life lessons on this plane must have lifted her a notch, because she certainly had an extraordinary ability to lift others. Her influence was wide. I'm certain I will write about this later. But back to the house.

In the haze of these days I can recall these things: endless conversations with my brother, and an outpouring of the things Mum didn't understand about me; as though it really matters now, and rifling through letters and boxes; the stench of urine in the library; and feeling like this cannot be true.

I look at her poetry collection like I will find the answer and I have a deep-seated need to share some of her favourites with the children I work with, but wonder at the Britishness of her collection, and so its relevance to a multicultural generation, and who own so much Chinese plastic, phones, and brash bling. Why would they care about Charles Causley and Eleanor Farjeon? Perhaps I have to show them, and this might get me through the days ahead.

I struggle to look at the photo albums but their relevance looms large as we try to agree on a collection of images and words to share with the 80 family and closest friends we decide to collect at her side for a goodbye. My mother will have an intimate gathering—a woman who could fill a theatre will get a service. Let's make sure the words and feeling are right. I have half an eye too on packing the smallest bag for an expedition to Japan. I pinch myself. What am I doing? But I feel very little. Only gratitude for the strength of community she showed us, that had slipped into an outer ring as her mobility and hearing faded, but was still true.

I find myself looking over and over at her angry notes and lists, mostly financial. I also feel let down. Let down by a family shake-up that tries to overshadow our farewell to Mum. As I look back at all the photos Mum looks like a radiant magnet and I suddenly see the truth in what looks back at me. Not every photo shows authentic joy.

I find myself wishing I had a faith and want to involve the synagogue in her blessing. Her rabbi clearly knows her but his daily work takes priority. We are not his missionaries. I am lost. I turn to the house once more for clues. I would suggest I begin in the office. It knows her best, but any tour guide would know that we should plan a route around the property. I have no idea where to begin, but all good visitors must powder their nose, so I step into the downstairs toilet, where I am greeted by paraphernalia so typically my mother's, and not touched for many, many years. This includes a little stack of books, in case you are planning a long visit. Books on manners and etiquette and a few jokes. The toilet, an old yellow one, is cranky and outmoded, has a fluffy lid that must be housing a family of bugs, and in front of me, a framed page of a sun bleached newspaper. I connect this room with Pears Soap. On my left, two golden dolphins try to hold a toilet roll. As in the last twenty years of their duty, the moment I touch the roll, they separate and the loo roll falls off. I smile. Mum, you are funny. Were.

I am not a great reader. I am not clever. Observant but not an academic. The house is filled with books, literature, the classics, the greats, and Mum collected Folio Society editions. Each birthday, my children were gifted the greats, often with a gold edge to the pages. I faked a thrill. I have successfully supported, with the help of a clever man, the education of two Russell Group graduates, both with keen abilities alongside their love of creation. Of that, I am proud. But me?

To sit in Mum's library is to observe all the books I never read, all the knowledge not absorbed, all the opportunity that gathered dust. I know why. It was a lack of engagement.

I look for clues in this room. I hear a childhood echo.

"What should I read?"
"A Square of Sky."
"Will I like it?"
"Well, it's like Anne Frank. The same story."

Mum goes off to continue her work with children. In the other room, I hear them laughing and chattering. Do I want to learn about death and war, or do I want to watch children a few years my senior re-enacting some duologues from some selected works? I choose the living over the dead. I will always choose interaction rather than dusty pages. I leave my dad to sleep on his leather chair. He is unwell. He sleeps with his mouth open. His tongue is peculiar. I never learned why, but it used to fall from his face as he slept. His psoriasis makes me uncomfortable and I wonder if we are the cause of his stressed condition.

To detect in this space is a great deal of work. I begin with a smell. My nose is good, and I recognise the dust and also the Mr. Sheen that is used to disguise it. The books are clustered, and I have some favourites still. Mum was passionate about theatre costume, and some of the books lean into her love. There is a collection here of spine-broken children's classics—Puss in Boots, Cinderella, and others—and I know the font in these slim volumes. Many biographies and... wait. I find a clue. My father's corner. His guides to antiques. He had tried to teach me a little about clocks. It seemed such an old man hobby. I have no idea who taught him. I see I gave him no credit for his journey from working-class Ilford to middle-class Berkshire, where he bought this extraordinary home, with no idea how to maintain it. But love, love drove him here. This collection, his and hers, doesn't really cross over, but they do show an ability to love. So there WAS love. Alongside neglect. An odd juxta positioning of care and non-care. I look properly at the shelves for the very first time, like I'm new to earth. I want to catalogue the name of every book on the shelves.

Mum has hundreds of children's poetry titles - The first I notice is Words on the Wind, then the spine of Bucket of Fish, and Nine O'Clock Bell— it all seems meaningless. I know this collection so well, but I begin to ask what is hiding on the top shelves of this room I believed I knew? In fact the reason I haven't a clue is that I was forbidden to stand on the surfaces and there is no other way up!

I am drawn to Russian Wonder Tales - perhaps a nod to our Polish-Russian Jewish heritage; The King's Own— there was never a mention of any interest in the monarchy. - only their sumptuous costumes; a book entitled Odd People—well yes, indeed that seems fitting; and Froggy's Little Brother by Brenda something-or-other— which might be worth a look. I believe thought that her interest in many of these titles was purely due to the gorgeousness of their gilt spines. But at last I spot my mum's influences - Brighton and Hove Official Guide; The Wallace Collection General Guide; Five volumes of Service of the Synagogue, including Passover, New Year, Tabernacles, and more; The Practice of Watercolour Painting by Baldry; Practical Camp Cookery for Guides by E.M. Anderson (she was a passionate girl guide which has always made me laugh as I never (and I mean never saw her walk even as far as the postbox and she certainly didn't take us camping; My only childhood foray into sleeping out was in covering the swing frame with pink blankets and sitting inside it until we heard leaves rustle, then running very fast into the house and slamming the door to keep the wolves out. An Adventure for Five Pence by Margaret Lovett; The Story of Jeanne d'Arc (a nod to strong women) and How to Enjoy Your Operation which sits alongside J.M. Barrie's Courage.

I can begin to sense mum in the room. I search the internet for clues about Froggy's Little Brother. It turns out to be the story of a seven-year-old froggy who strives to take care of his little brother after their parents have died. A laughably huge collection of frogs used to monopolise the kitchen but we've removed them. Mum - you are watching.

Time for a lolly. I'm off to the freezer. Some keep their freezer in the kitchen, and a few in the garage. Our family freezer sits in a room we call the Trunk Room. This room now houses the electric meter, the Henry hoover, and the cushions from the garden, all oddly bagged up in bin liners. I have no idea why.

Our house has some strange rooms: the Trunk Room, the Dwarf Room (I'll explain later), the library, the drawing room, the costume rooms, the theatre, the waiting room, and the front and back studio. These names have lasted long after the last of her students grew up and moved on, either to their one and only job as an actor in TIE on a touring bus, at C&A, or, for the "specials" (and there were plenty), on the world stage or winning their BAFTAs. There was no separation in our lives. Success was success. It was defined by: "Are you using what you learned, and does it make you happy?"

The Trunk Room has its own quirks, like the strange circle in the door that turns to let the air in. Or out. The smell of rusty nails, old hoover parts, marmalade tins without lids, and a broken spanner permeates the room. But the glory is in the handwritten labels marking the broken plastic drawers of old fuses, nails, and the indefinable. Through the handwriting, I can turn back time. My dad had amazing writing. It's not a skill we learn anymore, is it?

The Trunk Room once held one trunk, but it was a glorious one, and something I envied. It also held a sense of sadness for me. My sister went to boarding school, and her trunk, filled with midnight feasts, would have lived in this room, or extended cupboard, during the long holidays. I think I missed her during term time. I say "I think" because in truth, I can't remember. She is ten years my senior, and my memories are in birthday cards she made for me, framed in a sweet that looked like coloured glass, called Spangles, and really not much else. My sister and my older brother were absent for much of my childhood. My brother left home at fifteen and was rarely seen since. In fact, I can recall only one Christmas spent together, one Boxing Day when we shared my late father's birthday, and one shared family birthday three months before Mum died.

I know I'm bouncing around the spaces – I would make a dreadful estate agent. Some call it being light and bright on my feet, and my mother regularly remarked that I don't stick at anything. But now, I head through the back door – the one the postman uses – down a trip step and up another, and into the "back studio" which sadly no longer resembles the air raid shelter I used to love for its naughty "outside of purpose-ness." This studio, which is far too small to rehearse in, far too hard to fouette in, and far too cramped for Marie Kondo, sits above a cesspit. Yet it still reminds me of all my childhood making with enamel, wax, jewelry, and plastics, whose smells were banned from the kitchen, making them an isolated and isolating pursuit. It also returns me to my own perfect, gloriously pointless secret club, of which I was the self-appointed co-Director, along with my old-fashioned and able-to-keep-a-secret friend, the owner of Fergus the dog and sticky back plastic, Miss Fiona Beckett. Fiona and I were firm friends – we would have tea in her outhouse among the smell of fragrant flowers and homemade Victoria sponges, listening to her father's whistle coming from their cellar.

To me, this family represented the finest things in life – glorious summers, a first-class lawn with stripes to match her much older brother's shirts, tea, and tennis (which I did not play, having never been taught the basics). Fiona left me to go to boarding school, a very long way away. I later learned it was seven miles to High Wycombe!

But I lost my club, my sleepover buddy, and my clubhouse became redundant. I was surrounded by people but lonely.

crouching from wizards

A sharp sting
I pop
a drop
of blood
like a paper cut but made
from glorious green broken bottle glass
dug up with a twig
and borrowed from Mr and Mrs Worm
and gifted back
when tea is nearly ready.
I need to (pretend to)
wash my hands,
But I just can't,
because
I want to hold onto the fragile possibility that
I've found treasure
that might be lost
on a Roman road so
I bury it deep,
deep under that tree
-where we play
"Fairies and Wizards",
"Kiss Chase" with Christopher,
and gawp at Rodney's blotchy legs
as he clambers up the tree.

-where I sneak out my Nesquik
And tip it in my half-pint
(Mum says I can if I hide it
because the smell of milk
makes me gag
probably because I wasn't breastfed,
(but who knows)

and Mrs. Lewis says we need it
every single day
for our bones to grow
strong like Goliath
And maybe that's why I'm still little,
but big enough to forage
for jagged jewels in the soil.
After school there's white iced buns
and then we run across the road
to my house on a mission
to collect wallpaper rolls
and on the back we stick
leafs and crisps and hair
and make a world to share,
and then you are gone
so I climb inside
and share eternity with the mermaids
while you might be watching telly
with your dad
and mine is sleeping
and I imagine

all the village
chatting enthusiastic
round their tables
while I put on my static nightie
and chatter to the sky
before packing up the memory of copydex
and smiling at the seas we made
of leaves and fluff
and heading off to bed
and I look across the rooftops
to the spot our game began,

where I was small enough to crouch from the wizards.

heart beat - a song

There's
a little girl
on a swing
that won't fly
cause its held
by a pig
in a poke.

Still her hands
hold the rope
she looks down
at the soil
and she clings
to the day
that her smile
went away
and she hears
a door slam
and she moves
her small hands
to her eye
and the sky
falls in.

Little nails
you will grow again.
Little heart
you will show again.
Little girl
you will sing again.
Little girl
you will fly again
and so so high
with your knowledge
of the sky
and the joy
of the wind
you will swing
on your swing
to the skies.

High highest high.

from a glass bottom boat

You are transparent now,
and where you stood
to stir your coffee
is nothing
but what you
stood for.

In the living room,
if I screw my eyes tight,
I might glimpse an outline
of you
living.

You showed me a tiny tank,
and how to dream of multicoloured seas
from a glass-bottomed boat.

One day I hope to gaze into a reef
and see your face
and you might wink a wink
and smile a smile,
and I can wish
and I will know
which fish
is you.

I'll spot a bit of lipstick
on your tooth,
and you might swim
around me,
and I to you.

the place we used to know - a song

It isn't there now, isn't fair now,
Turning circles in the mare now,
Don't despair now, is it what we need to grow?

Don't be mad now, just be sad now,
Let the leaves fall off the tree,
Give it space now, not a race now,
What is meant is meant to be.

It isn't there now, isn't fair now,
Turning circles in the mare now,
Don't despair now, is it what we need to grow?

Don't be mad now, just be sad now,
Let the leaves fall off the tree,
Give it space now, not a race now,
What is meant is meant to be.

Don't be mad now, just be sad now,
Give it space now, not a race now,
What is meant is meant to be.

It isn't there now
Isn't fair now
Turning circles

in the mare now
Don't despair now
Is it what we need to grow?

Don't be mad now
Just be sad now
Let the leaves fall off the tree
Give it space now
Not a race now
What is meant is meant to be.

gold silver bronze

Golden years.
I spent so long sinking
Into cushions on
The right side
Of a closed door.
As times changed,
We swapped people for paperwork,
And the door
Creaked proudly into that space
And grew
An open door policy
Where there had always been an open door,
And we chose that for it.
It kept the door open.
Silver years.
I let them in to safety,
Remaining in control,
Deciding who could enter
And who might leave.
That door
Rattled when you danced.
It wasn't your right,
Nor yours for the taking,
But we opened it
And welcomed you in,

And you called it
Home.
You can dance now,
So you dance through your pain,
But me?
I am emptying boxes—
Symbols of things long gone:
Gold medals,
Silver medals,
Bronze bar.
Bronze.
Still pushing my limbs into empty air,
Trusting the molecules
To catch me as I fall.
I wanted this,
This time.
Then,
My body, my time,
My free flow.
And now?
Slam.
I am still alive.
Slam.
I am sorry.
Slam.
I can survive this
Through imaginings.
I imagine I can peep through the letterbox
At the dancing feet;

A family will now be having tea
At my dining table.
Slam.
My bedroom window.
My Snoopy sticker
Scratching away my childhood.
Like a scraper board
That I drew into
On those long "mum's working" nights,
Creating my stories in the black,
Making fairy dust
With a sharp tool
To mark the card
And mark my weekend.
Sat on the loo,
Deep in thought with Schulz—
An emblem of the meeting point
Between childhood and irony.
His memory,
A faded window sticker,
Is all that is left now
That I find myself.
I find myself on the wrong side
Of my own front door.
The phone no longer rings.
It is cold—
Like snow is cold.
Her voice.
The Readibrek glow

And the blackberry mittens
Have left me now.
"Just say you don't know."
Hot breath in my chilly bedroom
On waking.
I survived the cold
And the rusty water
And the summer of '76
And...
I spent so long on
The right side.
It was magic.
It was home.

One door closes…